King of the Jungle

Poems
by

Zvi A. Sesling

Selected as a 2008 PEN New England "Discovery" Reader
First Prize Winner 2007 Reuben Rose International Poetry Competition
Introduction by Sam Cornish, First Poet Laureate of Boston, MA

Copyright 2010 Zvi A. Sesling

Published by

Ibbetson Street Press
25 School Street
Somerville MA 02143

617-628-2313
www.ibbetsonpress.com

ISBN: 978-0-578-05136-9

King of the Jungle

Poems

by

Zvi A. Sesling

In memory of my parents

Meyer & Nechama Sesling

and

For my wife

Susan J. Dechter

Acknowledgements

Grateful acknowledgement is made to the editors of the following publications in which some of the poems appeared, some in slightly different form:

Bagel Bards 3, Chaffin Journal, Chiron Review, Eden Waters, Endicott Review, Ibbetson Street, Illya's Honey, Istanbul Literary Review, Journey, Main Street Rag, Midstream, Muddy River Poetry Review, New Delta Review, Saranac Review, Ship of Fools, South Boston Literary Gazette, Third Wednesday, Timber Creek Review, Touchstone (Viterbo College), The Tower (Canada), Voices Israel Anthology, WordWrights, Words of Wisdom

Special thanks to Sam Cornish and Doug Holder for their ongoing support, Molly Mattfield Bennett for editing and Susan Dechter for her editing and encouragement.

Cover art: #34 (16" x 12") by Irene Koronas

Cover & interior Design: **ISCS**press

Contents

I
Night time is a nightmare alone

Louis XVI's Last Thought	2
Shroud	3
The Kiss	4
Grammar	5
Moonlight	6
Mirror, Mirror	7
Nightmare	8
Ocean	9
Sheets Are Changed Weekly	10
Immigrant	11
Crossing The Yellow Brick Road	12
Flying Home	13
You Emerge Victorious From The Maze You've Been Traveling In	14

II
Words are sheets hanging to dry

Her Smile	16
The First Girl I Kiss	17
Untitled Love	18
King Of The Jungle	19
Eden	20

III
a storm rises like the moon

Saginaw	22
Argument	23
Something Better Left Unsaid	24
What It Takes To Say Goodbye	25
Witch	26
Dark Of The Soul	27
Gone	28
Photograph Of My First Girlfriend	29
Divorce	30
Dream In A Bottle	31
Last Stop	32
Like Knots On Counting Ropes	33
Lost Love	34

Lovers Dance	35
Old Friends	36
Lovers Quarrel	37

IV
hearts are for those who care

Tommy Eats Charisma	40
The Neighbor And The Oak Tree	41
The Lion	42
Untitled	43
Clinging Vine	44
Monet's Haystacks	45
Boredom	46
Black Snow	47
Black and White and Blue	48
Back Alleys	49
As Good As Dead	50
Archeology	51
Pyramid	52
Poet	53
TD Pass	54
Puzzle	55
Secrets	56
When I Get There	57
Wine Glasses And Bats	58
Withered Hand	59
Café Terrace	60
Wizard of Oz	61

V
The eye has seen too much, not enough

Dialogue	64
Fish Eye	65
The Final Tune	66
What They Did	67
Vietnam Memorial	68
What Armies Learn	69

VI
In the end the drawbridge was up

Drawbridge	72

Introduction

Zvi Sesling is a buttoned-down Bukowski — direct, honest male writing — who promises to be an authentic voice in poetry. By exploring the images of common realistic experience, he sometimes reveals more than he should. However, *King of the Jungle* profits from that because the poet opens himself up to the reader. As the title suggests, the writing is ironic and opinionated; therefore fresh and unpredictable. He speaks in a variety of male voices, all of them taking no prisoners. You don't have to like him and he doesn't care whether you do.

King of the Jungle avoids the clichés of other first books of poetry: he is neither confessional nor brave. He has the good sense to know that courage is not be found in poetry unless it is self-regard or social statement; the latter best shared in the confessional or with the Rabbi. These poems are about men and women — dark fantasy, noir and other themes found in serious humor and popular culture. How wonderful to discover folk poetry and fantasy in a poet who does not read *The American Poetry Review* or *Poetry Chicago* but rather the literary press. This is a writer who is under the influence of the poetic underground, Charles L. Grant and Philip K. Dick, laughing at yellow brick roads and the dark hiding beneath the bed or waiting behind the closet door. Some of these poems should be read before nightfall, when the only comforting sound is the bones creaking in your knuckles.

Sesling is a reader of poetry who has learned from the poets he admires and dislikes. This book comes not out of the classroom but rather from the author's life and imagination. At times I found myself enchanted — reading line-for-line with pauses and taking a deep breath before moving on. There are fragments of the poet's life but *King of the Jungle* is a first book by a writer who is losing himself in the word, in search of truth in a world he understands and has misunderstood.

Sam Cornish
First Poet Laureate for the
City of Boston, Massachusetts

I
Night time is a nightmare alone

Louis XVI's Last Thought

Okay so we have a fight over some silly thing
Not unusual for two people used to fighting

So I go to the florist and buy a dozen newly guillotined
tulips to give her, which she throws on the floor

Crushing them as if she were doing a Mexican Hat Dance
Or perhaps a Flamenco Dance, the heels clopping on the linoleum floor

And that gets me thinking about Louis XVI's last thoughts as his head
Is placed in the U-shaped slot, his hands tied behind his back

The cheering crowds like a modern day rock concert
Waiting for the string of his neck to be snapped in two

The cord is pulled, the scrape of metal on metal as the blade whirs
Its way down and Louis XVI thinks *merde*

The people cheer some more, common people, in their *liberte* joy
Loving the demise of the elite, their hands raised to God

Louis XVI's head is now in a basket while blood flows, the crimson tide
Of *fraternite* soaks the stage of *equalite* on which the play has acted out

While she in the kitchen trampling on my pride and apology
Orders me to clean up the mess she made

And I wonder who cleans up after Louis XVI, who takes the head
From the basket and places it back on its royal owner

Shroud

It all makes sense now
people walking around with

a shroud cloaking
their fear: crossing

a street where a car will hit them
or maybe a safe will drop from the

22d floor and squash them the way
they would step on a bug

or a gunshot will ring out and
stop their life, wreck happiness

will the spider's web of seduction
snare them or will they be a

mannequin in the window of Macy's, the red
star hanging above them like a Heineken logo

a light on the way to shopping
or a bargain basement chance at life

The Kiss

You kissed the brain with ideas
and the mouth with an east wind

There! A sculpture of David, a
painting of the Madonna

Somewhere an empty room
searches for you, an empty bed waits

The sky at night has no boundary
the stars appear in your smile

The world cannot contain your joy
the house empty without you

Bright eyes light the way
inner forces bring happiness

Grammar

The verbs on your tongue are hard to swallow
Adjectives in your ears are pleasant
Nouns in your eyes can be seen yards away
Why must you eat conjunctions

In the paragraph of one year
the sentence of love repeats itself
you punctuate it

Oh, how people love weekends
and love on weekends
how weekends make love

Thanks to a period everything stops
what stops ends
what ends is complete

Moonlight

I am sitting in my old rocking chair
on my lap is a solid book, thick with words

like coffee grounds the picture of the author on the
back cover, his hair, his face and five o'clock shadow,

pipe between his teeth steaming smoke like a winding road,
all of it lit by moonlight streaming in the window as if it were

a flashlight directed toward me, the full face of the moon trying
to decipher the words on the pages while I think that if the moon

can read, then this book about space ships and aliens was written for it.
On other nights reading is not an option because the moon is scimitar shaped,

offering little light, just a big grin in the gaping mouth of the night sky.
Other times the moon beckons, like the day man walked across its acne face,

kicking up dust like loose tea leaves in a cup. As it wanes and waxes
I sit in the rocker and watch the imperceptible movement toward darkness

or light wondering if we or some other civilization has made a base by which
the eventual control of the Earth becomes a reality rather than the material of

science fiction, which I am sitting here reading by the light of the full moon,
wondering what else moonlight brings.

Mirror, Mirror

The mirror is not cracked
it is the lines in the face

The mirror is not pitted
again, the marks are on the face

That is not dust on the mirror
it is just old age

There is no halo in the mirror
it is the bare light bulb's reflection

Those are not bugs crawling on the mirror
it is the past coming back

Those are not moths dancing on the mirror
it is the future attracted to the present

The mirror is made of real glass
it shatters the way lives do

Nightmare

Walk with padded feet
shoes of cotton and duct tape
socks of spider silk and lemon zest
for the earth opens, ready to swallow

Watch out for the dark where demons lurk
vampire dogs that smell you coming
cats that have not been fed in days
horses galloping to escape carnivores

Welcome the sun and its diseases
deny the moon its sad face
do not worry about being swallowed
the earth always gives up its dead

Ocean

It is not the way the moon lights
the watery highway from shore to infinity

It is not the waves flapping their
wings to avoid the rocks

It is not the fish that come up to
shake hands at the boat's rail

It is not the mermaids disguised as
seaweed waiting for the sea to set them free

It is not the blue of sapphire or the
sparkle of diamonds on the water

It is not the child splashing in the
place of his birth

It is the mother calling her children
her milk of foam bursting bubble

by bubble, her voice echoing in the
distance, roaring at us, taking us

home with no warning, a yanking
downward into the past, to the beginning

Sheets Are Changed Weekly

Satie never cleaned his sheets. They grew black and no woman would enter his bed. We do not know how often he bathed. But he played the piano well.

Sometimes in bugs I see wings that will take me to the house of the gambler where living on the wall I will learn his secrets.

With you I rarely win. It is never worth the gamble to lose a sure thing for the sake of pride or foolishness. So the sheets are changed weekly and the piano remains closed.

Immigrant

Just off the boat wearing
used clothes, cooking
borscht, sewing in a
sweatshop.

When the moon rises
fangs extend and there are
wistful looks at passersby.

Don't believe in vampires
she tells her son, they do not
exist. But just the same a
string of garlic hangs in the
kitchen to ward off the possible.

Night time is a nightmare alone
in bed with sounds of sex through
the walls where the newlyweds
moved into the apartment next door.

Crossing The Yellow Brick Road

There never was a yellow brick road
just a painted floor on a movie set

She (you know who) never landed in Oz
never left the farm in Kansas so there was never

An adventure, just a mushroom – or corn mash
induced dream

After all, lions and scarecrows and tin men do not
talk, that is reserved for two-legged wolves or the

Ones that want Red Riding Hood, men not
animals, dried grass or tin cans

No sir it is wolves that chase little girls, big bad
two legged ones to watch out for and you know what,

It is about seducing a thirteen year-old (or younger)

They are all in disguise, all pretending to help
all ready to pounce, hey a little corn mash helps

Those farm workers – three men – out there miles
from anywhere with pigs and cows and Auntie Em,

Face it, they want their fun and she is available so
what the hell, some stories end that way

Flying Home

We were supposed to fly home via
Phoenix, but due to a delay we fly

through Las Vegas. Out one side of
the airplane is water and an intrusion

of land stabbing it in the side. Out the
other side are mountains, their peaks

like hands raised, a small child answering
the teacher's question and a lonely beige

road pouring down from the hills into a longer
gray line that leads to a city where red and black

roofs top white houses and remind me of the song
Ticky-Tacky while people bustle around ignorant

of my existence on this airplane, probably not even
looking up from their busy Wednesday chores to

notice the airplane overhead, except for the little boy
whose balloon has slipped through fingers and as he

watches it bob and weave upward, catches a glimpse
of silver and studies the plane, perhaps wondering

why it does not leave a white trail as the plane, fifteen
thousand feet high heads for an unknown destination does.

He quickly turns back to the safety of his mother who
watches him as she speaks on the cell phone not knowing

that up here, thousands of feet above her and her son, I am
using a far more ancient form of communication. All this

as I think about a layover in Las Vegas where I can sit at a table
and communicate without writing or speaking. One finger

touching green felt tells the dealer to give me another card,
while a wave of the hand means no extra cards for me.

You Emerge Victorious From The Maze You've Been Traveling In*

Like a secret garden behind a Victorian home
Lost among bushes and trees
Turning a corner only to find more corners
Paths leading to dead ends

People passing with blank faces
Empty stares of yearning
Hands feeling ahead as if
The follower is blind or in the dark

Pathways of pebbles give hope
Yet lead nowhere except deeper into
The hidden world of lost rabbits and mice
Where no birds alight

Groping for a leaf with no meaning, no direction
A branch points the way out
Is it forgotten reality
Or is it subterfuge

An end with no meaning
A meaning with no end
Like a book with no pages
A song with no sound

Up ahead there is an opening
Beyond the opening an exit
You emerge victorious from
Maze you've been traveling in

*Title taken from a fortune found in a
 Chinese fortune cookie

II
Words are sheets hanging to dry

Her Smile
For Susan J. Dechter

I can hear her smiles in waves across
miles of telephone wires bringing

her voice and that smile unseen to warm
a cold room like a flame reaching outward

against the chill or lighting a darkened room
like a lamp touched with electric life. Her

voice and smile arouses my drowning spirit as
if she had tossed a raft into a sea of boredom

The First Girl I Kiss

I suppose most guys never forget
the first girl they kiss

It is an important passage in one's
life and mine was in Youngstown, Ohio

Where snow turned black from the steel
mills in just a few hours and blizzards

That brought the snow blew across Ohio
with cold wind that made you wish

For those hot, sweaty summer days when
it was perfect to be at the ball park in a

T-shirt and jeans, a cold Coke and a hot dog
in either hand watching Herb Score on the mound

Throwing pills past the hitter and Rocky Colavito
the idol of every Ohio kid who knew anything about baseball

Then that terrible line drive off Gil McDougal's bat
that essentially ended Herb Score's career, followed by

Rocky Colavito's trade to the Tigers putting a curse
on the Indians that even moving from Municipal Stadium

Could not undo, and just as suddenly as the shot that
took out Score, you break up with the girl of the first kiss

So my best friend moves right in and gets an even
better memory of first sex

It keeps going from there, I move out of town
ripped from everyone like the earth splitting

Forced to recover in a new town with a new girlfriend
While the Indians pursue their first World Series win since 1948

Untitled Love

Flies circle the head in anger
The tongue spits darts

Words are sheets hanging to dry
The mother has sent the child to school

She prepares for a lover's arrival
In solitude there is peace

Afterglow is the satisfaction of need
She will end her day the way it began

Dreams will fill her

King Of The Jungle

On a TV show there was an
orangutan, king of the jungle

the females would come to him
lie on their back and spread their legs

it is a law of the jungle – king
orangutan gets the females

in the human species looks, money
and sometimes personality could get

a female to lay on her back, spread
her legs and say *Enter my jungle*

And what a jungle! The vines wrap
around you, the lions roar

zebras cross the river as
crocodiles close in for a meal

monkeys leap in the trees and you
dream of the woman on the TV screen

Eden

A tree grows alone in the desert
by a cool spring where a man and
woman, naked, eat the fruit of the
tree, when from a cloudless sky,
lightning splits the tree into two
perfect halves and the man and
woman drop the fruit and leave
their paradise.

Crossing the desert they are scorched
by the sun, thirst has parched their lips
and throats so they cannot speak of
their tribulations and their skin has
darkened, their feet bleed, yet they
continue their journey until they stumble
upon an oasis, a small pool of water where
they drink and eat dates from a lone tree
and lay down together to sleep in each
other's arms having found Eden.

III
a storm rises like the moon

Saginaw

We look each other in the eye and it's no use
    --Jean Seberg, Breathless

It could have been in Saginaw
or Chattanooga, Dubuque

or Murfeesboro. One day they looked
at each other and knew it was over,

knew she would head west or south,
he would go east. Nothing to say –

words not necessary. She packed and
took a bus. He did not watch, did not want

to know where it was headed. He has forgotten
the day and the time. It is better

that way. There will be others they can look
at and see something – deep in the pupil

a camera lens will open and record beauty
or light – and a smile. Saginaw will fade, a pin

prick on a map, a page in a book, a thought
no longer remembered.

Argument

The heart is on the tongue
wagging like a dog's tail

Words hang out like
laundry to dry

Wet words from the
faucet of the throat

Pour out in hot anger
flow into the sink of the heart

Remember the good times
a boat making its way upstream

Something Better Left Unsaid

When mother died Beverly and I
were dating about a year and a half

It was not, I put it gently,
an idyllic relationship

She went to some adult experience college
for her Master's degree, which is to say

Adult experience is a substitute for never
earning a degree, much less attending college

Her Master's was in some kind of psychology
yet she could not shingle her door with a

Carefully lettered *Beverly, Psychologist*, an
All powerful sign that would bring up to $90 an hour

She did, however, like to practice her newly acquired
mental prowess on me, asking questions which she

Insisted I answer as I sat on the couch while she sat
in the stuffed leather chair rubbing her chin saying, *hmm, hmm*

As she imagined Freud doing, only she had no
chin hair to stroke, and one day as I recited childhood

Anxieties to help her write a paper for an amateur
psychologist magazine out of Durango, Colorado

She interrupted my recitation to ask, *What would you do
if I slept with someone else, you know, another man?*

She leaned back in her leather chair and let out a big sigh
like a balloon whooshing as the air escaped

And then her eyes fluttered shut and I knew our
sessions had come to an end

What It Takes To Say Goodbye

Goodbye is such a difficult word, more
Troublesome than a smile and quick hello
Like the day I saw you on the beach and you
Forgot you were topless and turned over to
See who was blocking the sun and there I
Was staring, slack jawed, you laughing at
Me, at my shock, your black hair splayed
Like a fan. The quick smile and hello a
Winning combo. You pulled something over
Your top and it was love at first sight. That
First night together you taught me tantric mantras
Or were they mantric tantras? Which ever, you
Abandoned them for a purple buzz hairdo and a
Navel stud, but still I loved you. Even when you
Put the eagle tattoo on your arm and another of a
Spider on your butt which moved when you were
Naked or wearing a thong bikini. Then you got
The pit bull and I began to get nervous and when
You brought home that two hundred and eighty
Pound biker with the leather vest, no shirt, with a
Beard, mustache and pony tail, and told me to sleep
In the basement where I could hear the springs in the
One hundred year old brass bed creaking to the load
Of the two of you, I knew our relationship changed,
And even more so when you told me – did not even ask –
Told me to make breakfast for you and Harley – can you
Imagine a biker named Harley? Anyway, that is when I
Discovered goodbye can be an easy word and maybe you
Ended up having to make breakfast.

Witch
--For B.R.

She is a witch without portfolio
driving a Corolla instead of a broom

turns a man's brain into Cream of Rice
his body pink with heat

soon he is like a dog, sitting up and begging
she tosses an occasional biscuit

then leaves the dog abandoned
while somewhere in Albuquerque another dog

has rolled over to have its belly rubbed,
only to be kicked by her passing fancy

Dark Of The Soul

A full moon lights
the dark of the soul

Prey trembles in the forest
the hunter stalks its prey

Do not stray from the path of light
falling like water between trees

Touching leaves like two lovers
kissing their way out

In the moon's shadow
darkness grows like a vine

Air escapes to another country
ceases playing its bassoon

In the silence of night
many things crawl

Gone

Abraham was going to sacrifice his son
I have gone one step further – cut him loose
Like a second round draft choice
To let him find a different coach, new role model
Released from the family team for the sake of my wife
Not really – for my own sanity

Abraham had his knife poised, waiting for the word
I had the words that cut into the heart
That stone cold organ where each beat
Drew further away – whose blood froze
Like water at the tip of an icicle
Like a stone in a dark cave
Forgetting sunlight and its origins

He is a name with no voice
A face with no meaning
A man's body with a boy's thoughts
An apple fallen too far

Photograph Of My First Girlfriend

Black & white photo
from a Brownie flash camera

white border and scallop edges
a white sleeveless dress

cat's eye glasses with rhinestones
a glue backed piece of paper is stuck

across the face I no longer remember
yet I still remember the first kiss

Divorce

Everything was agreed to:
division of property, child custody,

child support – even alimony!
So what happened? They hired lawyers,

suddenly everything got nasty, each side
upped the ante – they were not talking

to each other – rules were set down:
the house would be sold, the profits divided,

the child can be visited each Wednesday,
every other weekend, the alimony to be paid

by the 20th of each month. He cannot call before
7 am – 9 am on weekends nor on any day after 8 pm

She will have to buy a car, not use his and there will be
a coin flip to determine who picks first for the art work,

the loser to pick furniture first, including the piano and the
50" plasma TV, so the case goes into a contentious court

where lawyers will have to appear, so in the end the lawyers
make out well, walk out of court shaking hands, telling each
other

See you on the next case, while the separated couple head in
opposite directions, backs to each other, neither looking back.

Dream In A Bottle

He used to share her bed
They met at a party
No, her cousin introduced them
Forget those details

He told people she modeled
and he worked - it angered her -
she said modeling was work too
and he scoffed at the notion

He did not love her then and they
argued incessantly the subject
never really mattered just the
sense of fighting

He paid little attention to her
and she responded by leaving
finding a new home in a complex
with air conditioning and a pool

He sat outside her entrance with
a bottle and his dreams seeking
forgiveness and reconciliation
but instead she called security

He would not leave his post - or
his bottle - and her dates ignored
him when she took them to her apartment
and left him a dollar for his next dream

Last Stop

The world ended for him
in Salina or maybe it
began to close out in Cupertino

The day they left they argued – argued
all the way on Route 80 down 25 through
Denver and across Highway 70

She did not realize the dog was missing
until 100 miles to late – somewhere
in Kansas – so he told her it was probably

already adopted but she cried, saying it was
likely eating garbage – or even worse –
being eaten by a coyote

She was swearing up and down like an
elevator – her face red as Mars when they
stopped for gas in Salina

He escaped her wrath in the men's room and when
he came out there was a note on the gas pump:
Whatever happened to Bumpkins should happen to you

Like Knots On Counting Ropes

Like knots on counting ropes
we number the arguments
each a bit bigger than the previous

certain animals clash heads
when they disagree
we act more like parasitic vines

wrapping ourselves in words
which strangle our minds
like the death struggle we
fight to survive the scythe

a storm rises like the moon
slowly over the horizon
dark clouds scud toward us

rain falls and runs rivulets
through snow darkened by
age and exhaust fumes

sun always warms after
a storm like a mother's
touch after a fall

Lost Love

My lost love lives in Palo Alto
In a white stucco with a high
Narrow doorway like an arrow
Pointing up

She is married with
Three fat children like beach balls
And a bald husband, an accountant,
Who works seventy hours a week
To make enough to buy her the
Things she does not need

It could
Have been me married to her
Killing myself for no good reason

Bees do
The same for their queen and there
Is no love involved.

Lovers Dance

Not to music, but anger we quarrel
moving around each moving around
the coffee table, swaying through the
kitchen, back to the coffee table and
meeting between it and the couch
we embrace, forget our differences
before leaving for work, the dance
exhilarated you, exhausted me.
Next time let's tango.

Old Friends

What has happened to my old friends
Some have vaporized in saunas

Others have become autographs in
Someone's yearbook or on loose pages

There are those dead and desiccated
In the jungles or rotted in deserts

Some became statistics on highways
While others counted dollars as if

They were pebbles on a distant beach
The rest I look up to at night

Bid them farewell, make a wish
and join the waiting pillow

Lovers Quarrel

Words fly from the mouth
like bats from a cave at dusk

Form icicles of anger
pierce like an arrow

There in a state of gracelessness
the path winds into the wood

A dirt road that matches
the mood, purple blood rising

Like a kettle, steam condenses
on the wall, neighbors wear earmuffs

IV
hearts are for those who care

Tommy Eats Charisma

Tommy want to be a politician and the
Street walkers tell him he is too dull.

A doorman says he needs charisma and
Can get it at the deli around the corner.

For $3.95 Tommy gets a plateful of
Charisma with a side of gab.

Tommy devours it like a student reading
Playboy and runs out to campaign for City Council.

The girls on the street tell him he speaks
Too slowly and the doorman says the deli

Around the corner has a special on fast talking
So for another $3.95 he gets a bowl full of it

And a cup of facts to spew forth which gets
Him elected mayor and has the street walkers

Shipped out of town so he can claim his city is clean.
The doorman asks for a job and Tommy laughs

And tells him he did not contribute to the right candidate.
Tommy now wants to be governor and he stands on the

Corner sparkling charisma like fireworks, gabbing America,
Fast talking taxes like snake oil and offering facts

To a woman with a dog that bites him.

The Neighbor And The Oak Tree
-- for J.S.

The branches of the oak tree in my yard
grow over the fence providing you shade
and leaves to rake and occasionally, when
a blue jay lands heavily, a shower of snow
that comes down on you and junior as you
build a snowman while your dog barks, jumps
around as if laughing at you

So this spring when you knew I was not at
home you pulled the ladder I have not seen
you use in all the years we have lived next
to each other, you bought a saw which
I never imagined you knew how to use and
began that back and forth rhythmic motion
until all the branches on your side of the fence
were gone and with a smile of satisfaction you
put the saw and ladder away went out to eat

Cutting those branches off was like severing
my arm and the tree began to bleed until there
was blood in your yard, pools and puddles of
blood as the great tree cried washing the blood
into the ground causing last autumn's acorns to
sprout all over your lawn so you could not cut
them down fast enough and for each one you did
cut, two more came up until your yard looked like
Medusa's head and no one could look at your yard
or visit you for fear of turning to wood

The Lion
--for Edward M. Kennedy

The lion is at the gate
his silver mane
rattles with each roar

Past, present, future
shoot out of the mouth
like cannon balls against brick

Once feared, now revered
the long road has taken him
out of the jungle of words and promises

Scars of life and battles have wizened him
his pride now in himself, the roar
reserved for enemies – he has chosen his
battles and let his dream live on

Untitled

The long of it was the marriage
The short of it was the divorce

In between were two tales that
rarely told the same story

Marriage like a pair of flip-flops
One slapping ground, the other swatting air

Sand between the toes irritates
Sand fleas of discontent swirl around

And, oh, the salt water, how it burns open wounds
Healing begins, scars remain

Clinging Vine

He drags the clinging vine through the streets,
through the dust of unpaved alleys, her arms

wrapped around his leg. Her face is sweat and
running make up, her legs kick air.

People stare and do nothing. One woman smiles
sympathetically, men turn their heads and dogs

snarl. How did this happening come to
pass? There was once a scene in a movie. There

was a page-long paragraph in a novel. She learned
the lessons well: hang on with all you have, there

will be no help but sympathy will give you heart,
heart will provide strength and strength will help you cling.

Monet's Haystacks

In a field of wildflowers the young
girls stands staring out at Monet's haystacks.
She is picking flowers, has stopped to
contemplate the meadow, or is it indecision?
In a dream I lead her to the haystacks,
tell her of Monet, but she does not understand.
I pick flowers for her. She has placed a basket
beneath a tree and offers to share bread, cheese and wine.
We exchange pleasantries. I depart. In the morning
she is still standing in her field of wildflowers. Her look
now vacant as if it is indecision.

Boredom

He was drumming his fingers, raising
First the forefinger, then the middle,
Ring and pinkie, and dropping them
Rapidly to create a drumming sound,
Repetitious and as boring as he was
Bored, the only sound in the room
The incessant rat-a-tat-tat of the fingers
Matching the vacant look in his eyes, the
Falling of his face like a melting ice cream
Cone, his left ear cocked slightly upward
To hear a sound that would break the
Boredom, free him from the classroom

For Wanda Bowers, English teacher, Ret.
University City (MO) High School

Black Snow
Youngstown OH, 1956

Black snow, ashes
from the mills
Youngstown Sheet & Tube
Like weather measles
melting, cutting rivulets
to gutters

black snow
the labor of men
at the hot furnaces
in the cold winter
they face flame

filth of man
poison of toil
black snow
from the mills

Youngstown Sheet & Tube
gone now
black snow
forgotten

Black and White and Blue

Two women sit alone, opposite
each other like mirror images, both

in black blouses, pants, stockings and shoes
cigarettes in their mouths, smoke curling out

like gossamer snakes
their knees do not touch, they do not touch each other

they do not talk
both are very thin, so thin they could fit into a

bottle of Pinot Noir
their black hair is starkly pulled back

tied in a bun
their black eyes stare into space

The table they sit at is white
the wall is white, the floor is white

the light in the restaurant is white
the cigarettes are white

their moods are blue

Back Alleys

To find you I must navigate a maze
of back alleys, narrow with centuries

old wooden houses lining cobblestone
streets worn down and broken by years

of horse hoofs and wagons and a sky that
cries like the soon-to-be widow whose

husband is in captivity. The search goes
up a pinching of steps, around narrow bends

where no taxi can fit, down slippery slopes one
could ski without snow. Mice live in the spaces

between the stones despite children who try to
catch them with old pillow cases and peanut butter.

If only there were footprints to follow or a trail of
orange peels or pistachio shells. But like a ghost

you have vaporized and I follow the foggy memory
that fades as the sun rises.

As Good As Dead
    --for L.S.

Morning consists of lying in bed
    with talk radio

Breakfast is a bowl of cereal
    day is a clerical job
        for a government agency

The apartment is always a mess
    debt is the rubber hand
        that slaps back

Does not own a television
    dinner is a bowl of cereal

Night consists of lying in bed
    with talk radio

Not much else to do
    except sleep
        repeat the day

Weekends in bed
    with talk radio
        listen, listen

No one to talk to

Archeology

The dust of bones has mingled with
Sand, and the wind whistles a funereal
March of the ancients who rise from
Graves to tell their lives – the great of
Their time, greater three millennia later
When their names reappear on a stone
Tablet, the nameless are the sand that
Has been brushed from the stones. Ancient
Pottery has its tale for the trained, as do
Walls and bones and jewelry. Those who
Conquered have left their glory for all time
And the conquered, once thought obliterated
From the memory of time, have been
Resurrected and honored – king and slave
Equal in a future neither would have dreamed.

Pyramid

There among flat sands
the color of a cat
the grey pyramid rises
pointing to heaven
a single finger speaking
to a god forgotten
built by slaves forgotten
their names buried
with them forever
while the pharaoh
nameless for three thousand
years is found and
revered, his fame not
in the pyramid that rises
but supported by the
crushed Hebrew bones
beneath him

Poet
--for Doug Holder

Bald head covered by straw hat
grey beard trimmed

You once had black hair
and moustache, looked like

The cover of a 70s rock album
but now you sit in shorts

Sandals and a blue shirt
talking poetry, making mental

Notes, watching like a cat
watches a bird, your mind

A stalking machine, already
choosing words, your eyes

Absorbing features, a sponge
of thoughts squeezed through

a pen, the paper turning black
with drops of ideas

TD Pass

The wide receiver does his best to deceive.
A head jerk to the left, a hip to the right, a
bump off the defensive end, a turn and fake
on the safety.

Then man-on-man down field with the cornerback
practically snapping at his heels like a turtle.

He accelerates, as does his living shadow.
He cuts toward the sideline, so does his opponent.

Thirty yards behind them the quarterback has
spotted the target, lifted his arm, and with secure grip
throws the football like a missile at an unseen enemy.

The ball spirals forward cutting air as it rises, hurtles
toward the target and descends to outstretched arms.

The defender also reaching upward and forward with
one hand, tugs the receiver's jersey with the
the other, hoping a referee does not see the infraction.

Just behind the line of scrimmage the quarterback has been
leveled by a charging defender and lays smothered.

Underneath the weighty bulk of the linebacker, the quarterback
cannot see the results of his efforts, but the cheering tells him.

The ball has landed in the receiver's arms; the defender has failed
and his one hand cannot hold the speeding receiver.

The defender slips to the ground and the receiver races to
the end zone; no one close enough to deter him.

The crowd, on its feet, cheers and while the quarterback,
still on his back, issues a small smile of satisfaction, the
receiver wiggles a victory dance and flips the football to a
nearby referee.

Puzzle

The jigsaw puzzle is not complete
there are pieces in the box which
contained a life that includes an ocean,
a ship that brought her to port, the country from
which she departed, the child left behind
like a treasure chest to be recovered later when
no one is looking, the other child not quite able to
grasp it all or understand why there is an unkown
uncle, aunts never to be spoken to, cousins
who are ghosts of memories, stories spun from dreams
or netted like fish from vivid imaginations, tales to
deceive like an eclipse of the sun – a dark side
not to be looked at directly – a father's divorce
never mentioned, the first wife looking very much like the
second – were there two? More pieces, the edge of the puzzle
not smooth or straight as in a fairytale, the edges rough
like life, not sharp as a tongue. How did she get here?
By ship for sure, which ship – freighter rusting like a
waiting husband - the Queen Mary (or so she said), crammed
with refugees seeking hope, wealth, freedom, family in the
New Paradise while on the decks above the rich sat idly
speaking of matters the poor would not understand – or maybe
it was another ship from another country filled with languages
peeled from palm trees or evergreens or yakking as diverse as
birds overhead or in trees at dusk, the ocean a deep
blue-green, white foam off the stern a trail away from the past,
away from life as it was, the bow splitting water as if it were
thoughts pointing to hope while years later after her death holes
in the puzzle remain as unfilled as a hungry stomach

Secrets

What is true may not be true
it depends on the teller of the truth
For example: the man has told you
for most of your life that he is your
father and your mother is your mother
He tells you this repeatedly like rain
falling so you believe him because
you have no umbrella

Later in life, you discover he was
divorced, so the questions become:
was it before or after your birth – or
with which wife were you conceived –
were there other wives, are there other
children

He tells what he does for a living, yet
later, like boiling oil, secrets bubble up
that have been buried like gold to keep
Cossacks from finding it, stealing it,
leaving you empty handed like a beggar
seeking rubles or pennies for the next meal
Secrets you determine are his truths,
the rest is all lies – does it really matter?

When I Get There

When I get there it will be my parents who greet me
Father with his stern look, angry that I have learned
His harshness was more abuse than discipline.

Mother aloof as always, critical that I did not spend
More time in her company.

Grandfathers and grandmothers I never knew will try
To guilt me that I did not know them and their sufferings,
Nor pay attention to my father's lessons about them.

Piles of ancestors like old newspapers in the basement
Will present themselves like headlines for me to acknowledge.

Dogs from my past will bound forward through green fields,
Tails wagging a quick metronome to their happy bark.

My black cat, distant as my mother, will sit on a rock drinking
The sun, allowing himself the luxury of an occasional purr, the
Twitch in his tail, a signal of annoyance at being detected.

The sky will be a wondrous blue, like the aquamarine in my mother's
Ring, the sun, yellow like the stars my aunts, uncles and cousins wore

The green meadows will be filled like Noah's Ark with animals at play
With each other and there will be peace everywhere and respect for each
Person, and I will wonder why the world from which I came could not
Have been so, and glad I have been welcomed to this one.

Wine Glasses And Bats

Whoever invented the rack
that holds wine glasses at a

bar probably got the idea from
from watching bats hang upside down

Bats fly out of caves at dusk
to catch as many beetles, moths

and mosquitoes as possible
more than the bats' own

weight – the mosquito bloated
with human blood, carrying diseases

they pass on to birds and people are
scooped up by bats whose unerring

sonar detects the flying insects and
swallow the little flying creatures

who may have been celebrating a
hemoglobin meal only to suddenly

become the main course along
with all manner of flying insects

So bat guano used as fertilizer to grow
vegetables that feed people comes

from insects and mosquitoes that feed
off people, a cycle as sure as the seasons

when one enters a bar to have a cold beer
in summer or a glass of wine – red wine

like blood – to be sipped from a glass
hanging upside down waiting

Withered Hand

But for this withered hand
he could have steered a ship
to ports of call as different
as the colors of the native skins,
Or captained an airplane
through clouds to lands
of which he can only dream,
he could have raced cars,
or fought wars and conquered,
he could have ruled and had people
bend to my will with each edict
he issued and ordered read,
Instead, he has this withered hand
with which to teach so that others may
live what he can only dream

Café Terrace

If I could step into Van Gogh's
painting of Café Terrace with its
yellow lighting and lovers strolling
on cobblestone streets, the buildings
looming in the dark and the people
sitting at the café's tables with their
coffees, I should select for my table,
the one where the woman sits alone
trying to see her future in the swirl
of coffee and milk, in the grains of
sugar slowly sinking into the brown
murk. I would sit down without asking
her permission, say hello in English
with the hope she knew enough to
answer and I would order the same
drink she was having. I would tell
her of the beautiful sky, blue like the
collar around a king's cape and the
stars like popped corn. I would tell
her how nice it would be to stroll the
cobblestone streets until we were too
tired to continue and she could invite
me upstairs to her third floor flat where,
panting from exhaustion, I would fall
asleep waiting for the kettle's anxious
call. In the Café Terrace the woman has
no face, as so many other women I
have known.

Wizard of Oz

Heart, brains and bravery each
seeking entitlement, the welfare

Of fiction in the hands of a leader
Who seeks something greater

Hearts are for those who care, brains
belong to those who seek, while

Bravery is the reward of those without
hearts or brains, but abundant in instinct

The green skinned witch is an aberration
of the mind, a bad dream, an ex-wife

We seek answers and find only new
puzzles, our heads like a Rubik's

Cube of questions as confusing as a
Pollack painting – all splatters

V
The eye has seen too much, not enough

Dialogue

Two men are riding on a
crowded transport train to Auschwitz

One is already dead
the other is dying

The dying man says to the dead man
So, *what's it like being dead?*

The dead man answers *At first I was
cold, as you are, then everything*

*gray turned blue from the sun and my
heart melted from the beauty around me*

The dying man listened, closed his eyes
as if to dream and joined his new friend

Fish Eye

Once, in the home of a Filipino, I was
served soup with the head of a fish

floating in the middle, the eye staring up
as in a pile of the dead in

Auschwitz, the center of the eye forming
a question mark asking, *Why me? Why am*

*I here? What have I done to earn this infamous
plight?* The eye not only sees, it tells you

about surprise, shock, fear, anguish and pain.
You can still see love, but not happiness or humor.

The eye has seen too much, not enough.
Questions are answered, questions remain.

In the end humanity consumes fish
consumes humanity.

The Final Tune

Read this poem at a different pace,
A slow pace like a solitary solemn drum
At a funeral march. Read it as a dirge,
The measured tune of taps, the slow single
Tear making its way through desert heat
To the lips, where the salt accentuates
Bitterness. It is the poem of the wail
And the howl, the chest beating, the
Torn black cloth, the plain wooden
Casket and the final toss of earth. It is
The poem of death, of sadness immortal
In the heart at the final goodbye.
It is the poem of the senseless and
Needless death inflicted by hate
Carried out by petty mortals for a
God supposed to teach love.
The poem knows love for the
Dead, while the living learn the
Never ending song of sorrow.

What They Did

Ask Not What your country
can do for you, ask what you
can do for your country
        --Pres. John F. Kennedy
          Inauguration Speech
          January 20, 1961

So they listened to him, first they
went off to combat poverty, ignorance, illness
earned little, suffered for their country

Others fought the communist threat in the
jungles and died for their country, thousands dead,
thousands more wounded, maimed, psychologically damaged

Then another war, thousands
more dead and wounded – lost arms, legs, faces
they knew why they were there – they were doing it for their country

How much more can the young be asked to do?
How many presidents will ask them to do for their country?
How many of the young will not ask, but will die trying to do?

Vietnam Memorial
Washington, DC

Descend into America's hell
black wall rising like death itself
sinking lower, feeling depression push down
names, faceless names, stare back
through dotted i's and crossed t's
through curved c's and rounded o's
the names stare back
letters rearrange and ask,
'Why am I here? Why not you?'

There are no answers
never were
just names and tears
from those who stare
at the names

What Armies Learn

Clouds come in like
wet gray army blankets
squeezing water until
grass grows a foot high
and trees drop their nuts
to float away like a Roman
fleet to Carthage.
Weather and war are symbiotic.
Napoleon and Hitler learned
about Russian winters. America
did not survive Vietnamese
jungle rot.

Parasitic vines grew in his ears,
the camouflage was real and
he will be found like a Machu
Pichu mummy in three hundred
or a thousand years, a marvel to
the victorious digger.

VI
In the end the drawbridge was up

Drawbridge
In Memory of Alexandra Kaplan

Think of the drawbridge as two
Lives that rise and fall, two lives
Separate yet together, connecting
Different shores and spanning the
Dark waters below, cars crossing
Like people passing through our lives.

It was Alzheimer's she was told and
Her descent into the murky waters of
The disease began by forgetting friends,
Colleagues and relatives, drowning in
Forgetfulness, not knowing herself.

In the end the drawbridge was up,
Her life on one side, nothing on the
Other side, she at the pinnacle of
Northingness where the drawbridge had
Separated, leading her into the dark beyond.

Photo by Susan J. Dechter

ZVI A. SESLING has published poetry in numerous magazines among them: *Midstream, Poetica, Voices Israel, Saranac Review, New Delta Review, Plainsong, Asphodel, Ibbetson St., Haz Mat Review, Istanbul Literary Review, The Chaffin Journal, Ship of Fools and Chiron Review.* He was awarded Third Place (2004) and First Prize (2007) in the Reuben Rose International Poetry Competition and was a finalist in the 2009 Cervena Barva Press Chapbook Contest. In 2008 he was selected to read his poetry at New England/Pen "Discovery" by Boston Poet Laureate Sam Cornish. He edits the *Muddy River Poetry Review.*

www.ingramcontent.com/pod-product-compliance
Lightning Source LLC
Chambersburg PA
CBHW031209090426
42736CB00009B/844